HEALING THE HEART MINDFULLY

A Practical Approach to Holistic Rehabilitation from Cardiac Surgery

By Monica Jain

Healing the Heart Mindfully
A practical approach to holistic rehabilitation from cardiac surgery
By Monica Jain, PT, DPT

Editor - Ariel Kiley
Copy Editor - Debbie Volpe
Cover Page - Onward Publication
Photos - Emily Dryden

Designed by,
Choudhary Offset Pvt. Ltd., INDIA

TABLE OF CONTENTS

Introduction

SECTION 1 - MINDFULNESS

The Power of Mindfulness 1

What is Mindfulness? 1

My Story 2

SECTION 2 - MINDFUL TOOLS FOR YOUR HEALING JOURNEY

The Mindful Mindset 8

The Present Moment 8

Mindful Breathing 8

The Science Behind Mindful Breathing 9

Mindful Breathing Techniques - *Belly Breathing, Pursed Lip Breathing, Alternate Nostril Breathing, Optional Mantra Technique* 10

Listen to Your Body 13

Posture 13

Gratitude 13

The Mindful S.N.A.C.K- *SNACK in Action* 14

SECTION 3 - POST SURGERY IN THE HOSPITAL

Pain Versus Suffering 19

How to Break Through Pain 20

Movement and Rest 20

Movements Coordinated with Breathing 21

Avoiding Comparison and Trusting the Process 21

Mindfulness Beyond Recovery 22

Preparing for Home 23

SECTION 4 - GOING HOME AND OTHER CONCERNS

Exercise and Rest   27

Dealing with Home Demands   28

Complete Healing   28

My Vision - A New You   29

Conclusion   30

Testimonial - Mindfulness Post Surgery and Beyond   31

About My Journey, This Book and My Ongoing Work   31

APPENDIX - POST SURGERY PHYSICAL THERAPY

Sternal Precautions   35

Exercise Overview   36

Hospital Exercise Program   36

Home Exercise Program   40

Introduction

If this book is in your hands, you are probably curious about post cardiac surgery rehabilitation and mindfulness. Or you want to help somebody who is going through it.

Either way, you are on the right track!

The words "cardiac surgery" can be stressful. Post cardiac surgery is a tricky path. However, there is a way to make this path smoother, more positive, and peaceful. *It is called Mindfulness.* No challenge in life can affect your inner well being when mindfulness is the foundation.

My experience as a post cardiac surgery physical therapist for the past 16 years has inspired me to bring new insight into the journey of recovery. By combining mindfulness practices with physical therapy assessment and treatment, patients experience a more complete recovery and feel an extraordinary difference.

They not only recover physical health and mobility in order to return to their daily lives, but there is also a significant improvement in their quality of life and overall wellness after learning to use mindfulness.

I wrote this book in response to many requests from my patients, their families and surgery team, to write and share what I practice.

The information shared in this book is simple, clear and practical. It will help you navigate your journey through surgery with time-tested mindfulness techniques to stay calm, focused and grounded.

You will learn how to choose your mindset, incorporate mindful breathing techniques, and befriend your body to optimize rehabilitation after heart surgery. This valuable resource will help you become the architect of your own recovery, if you practice the shared information.

I invite you to empower yourself with this life-changing approach to holistic rehabilitation for your heart, body and mind.

Open the pages to let your journey begin........

Sending love your way,

Monica Jain

SECTION 1

Mindfulness

SECTION 1

Mindfulness

The Power of Mindfulness

When I first saw Mr. Z on day 2 after a coronary artery bypass graft, he was irritated and he adamantly refused to have a physical therapy session. He experienced a lot of pain while trying to get out of bed the previous day. He was annoyed with everyone who kept reiterating how important it was for him to get out of bed. So when I approached him, he said he might try later when the pain diminishes.

I understood where he was coming from. So, I decided not to try to convince him how a physical therapy session would help. Instead, I just requested him to try one mindfulness breathing exercise in bed in an upright seated position. He agreed to do it. After a couple of belly breaths, he was in a much calmer state.

Mr.Z could then tap into his own power. He agreed to try once to get out of bed. By coordinating breath with his movements, he not only sat at the edge of the bed, but also stood up slowly. He walked 200 feet with my assistance.

While walking with him, I kept reminding him about his posture and slow deep inhales and exhales. At the end of the session, he said it wasn't that bad. "I created the idea that getting up would be very painful even before I did it, because I was still in yesterday's experience. I not only felt less pain and discomfort but I also felt very confident after this session." This is the power of mindfulness.

What is Mindfulness?

Mindfulness is as simple as just being fully aware in the present moment. The **NOW** moment. Not suppressing any feelings, but working with them consciously here and now.

To be mindful means to be aware of thoughts, emotions and reactions, and to use that awareness in response to any situation. It is about being in touch with what is going on inside AND outside yourself through your connections with others, nature, and the environment. Mindfulness helps you develop a compassionate awareness of your thoughts and feelings, which in turn allows you to make more informed choices about the way you live your life.

When determining if mindfulness is for you, the questions to ask yourself are: Do you want to be a victim? Do you want to be passive in your recovery? Do you want to keep hoping that eventually you will start feeling better and wait around for that day to come? Do you want to get helplessly frustrated with challenging situations constantly increasing your stress?

OR...

Do you want to be a victor? Do you want to tap into your own power? Do you want to be the creator of your experience? Do you want to design your own empowering way of interpreting and responding to any given situation?

If you responded **YES** to the latter, then the right approach for you is mindfulness. No matter what obstacles you come across in your recovery phase, mindfulness practices will allow you to choose happiness, calm, and peace.

My Story

I know the power of mindfulness in tough times because I have experienced it firsthand. When my infant daughter developed severe eczema, her recovery was a slow and painful two year process. At that time, my mindfulness practice kept me grounded and guided me to operate from a place of patience, love and courage.

It was really hard to experience the pain that she was experiencing...the constant itching and the many sleepless nights. But looking back, I feel pride in saying I handled the situation powerfully. This gave me tremendous faith in mindfulness.

When I was pregnant with my second child, the first ultrasound revealed he had only one umbilical artery (normally there are two attached from the placenta to the baby). As a physical therapist, I knew how many abnormalities could happen with this child.

In the midst of all the worries and situations that were out of my control, I decided again to lean on my mindfulness practice, along with whatever else needed to be done from the medical side. When the time came, I had an easy delivery and my son was born completely healthy.

After these experiences with my two children, I knew mindfulness helped me become a victor in the midst of great challenges. Inspired by my own transformation, I decided to train to teach mindfulness to my patients and community. Upon seeing the incredibly positive results of combining physical therapy with mindfulness for my patients, sharing this work became my passion.

SECTION 2

Mindful Tools for Your Healing Journey

SECTION 2

Mindful Tools for Your Healing Journey

Once your surgery is complete, the biggest and scariest part is done. Congratulations! You are now in the post-operative phase. You have made it halfway through your recovery and are about to enjoy life more qualitatively.

Take a moment here to acknowledge yourself for coming this far. Pause, put a hand over your heart, and take a few deep breaths. Find a sense of gratitude for how far you have come. Your skilled surgeons have completed the most complicated part, the surgery. Thank the universe for creating them and feel grateful for their help. There are so many people who cannot even access medical services. Pause and appreciate the care you have received so far.

Here comes the next leg of your healing journey: **The Recovery Phase.**

The recovery phase is when you, the patient, take the lead and claim primary responsibility for yourself. Everyone else becomes secondary. By everyone else I mean **everyone,** including your doctors, nurses, therapists, family members, etc.

You are the one who is going to complete these final steps. Once you take responsibility, **everyone** will come together to support you. As you claim primary responsibility for your healing process, say this affirmation:

I want to get better.
I want to feel better.
I want to enjoy my life.
I am ready to give my best effort.

By declaring this positive intention from the start, you will create a whole different momentum in your healing journey. It is now time for you to do the work of your recovery. This will help you to enjoy all the goodness the surgery has brought. Remember, it is not just recovery for yourself, but for all of your loved ones. The following tools and techniques will empower you throughout the recovery phase. And you will need them to approach your recovery mindfully; to be the architect of your own experience.

The Mindful Mindset

When it comes to recovery, your mindset matters. Mindset is simply your mental attitude or a fixed set of beliefs. The experience of surgery - the anesthesia, medicines, and the post-operative course is enough to exhaust your body.

You don't need further stressors added to the list. Although you may not realize it yet, your mindset can block or limit your recovery.

If you welcome negative thoughts, worries and concerns, and continually choose to think about them, your precious energy will be drained. You will feel exhausted and unwilling to give one hundred percent, which is crucial during the recovery period.

My decade of experience has shown over and over again that you as a patient can significantly contribute to your recovery. You can use the recovery process to take your life to a different level, not only physically but as a whole human being as well. This starts with a positive, committed mindset. And most importantly, getting grounded in the present moment.

The Present Moment

I cannot emphasize enough how important it is for you to be mindful of the present moment. This is the recovery moment. If you dwell on the past or worry about the future, you tax your body and mind. You undermine this moment of potential healing right now. Many claim that it is easier said than done.

I want to be in the present moment but I have a hundred things going on in my mind. How do I do it?

When you feel overwhelmed, pause and check your thoughts. Notice if they are preoccupied with the past or future. Then harness your attention by focusing on your breath.

Mindful Breathing

The easiest way to bring yourself to the present moment is by taking a conscious breath. You breathe all the time, but bringing awareness to the breath is key. You can never breathe for the future nor for the past. You can only breathe in the present. Not only focusing on the breath can help you enter the present moment, but through conscious breathing, you can increase your body's own rehabilitative functions to keep your recovery moving forward.

Belly breathing (also called diaphragmatic breathing), in particular, is proven to create a calmer, more relaxed state by triggering your parasympathetic nervous system. Your parasympathetic nervous system is what helps your body rest and recover. You will learn more about this system in the next section.

Understanding mindful breathing techniques is easy. To practice them takes commitment. This is why I want you to choose to be the creator of your experience, instead of a passive bystander.

Repeat the affirmation:

I want to get better.
I want to feel better.
I want to enjoy my life.
I am ready to give my best effort.

There are several breathing techniques that will be discussed in the next section. Try them all out. Once you have practiced them, you will see the results and you won't have to remember what you read.

For example, I can tell you that an apple tastes great and you might believe me. But you can't really know how it tastes until you try it for yourself. Once you know, you will choose to reach for it on your own when you crave that flavor. It is the same principal with mindful breathing.

You must experience the breath work yourself. This mindful breathing work will help you tackle the most challenging aspects of your recovery from a state of peace and confidence.

The Science Behind Mindful Breathing

Your autonomic nervous system has two subsystems: parasympathetic and sympathetic. The sympathetic nervous system is responsible for fight or flight. It rules the stress response.

During a stress response, your heart rate elevates, digestion slows, and there is increased blood flow to the muscles in preparation for fight or flight. The parasympathetic nervous system is responsible for relaxation. What happens during relaxation? Your heart rate slows, digestion increases, and your body calms.

The vagus nerve, the largest nerve in our body, runs from the brain into the abdomen and is the major channel of the parasympathetic nervous system. The vagus nerve promotes relaxation, which counteracts the sympathetic nervous system.

Unfortunately, modern life triggers the sympathetic nervous system much more than the parasympathetic. Medical and physical impairments add stress on top of that. The all-too-frequent result of this imbalance is a body stuck in overdrive which can trigger chronic inflammation, the precursor to numerous chronic diseases.

While you can't control the stress response, since it's automatic, you CAN control the relaxation response. To do so, you must actively relax. This is where breathing and the vagus nerve come into play.

When you consciously engage in slow, belly or diaphragmatic breathing, you activate the vagus nerve. In turn, this acts as a balancing system to all that stress that has accumulated in the whole journey from the diagnosis to surgery to the recovery phase.

Even one conscious breath begins to activate your vagus nerve and kicks off a wonderful cascade of benefits. The heart rate slows, blood pressure drops, and the body enters a state of mental and physical calm. The vagus nerve is the hose that carries the water that quells the flames and restores your body to a non-emergency state.

Mindful Breathing Techniques

After reading these techniques, try them for 2-3 minutes and notice what happens. Discover your own experience. Look for an increase in peace, calmness, and stillness. Try to enjoy this moment of being present with the breath.

After using these techniques, your anxiety and nervousness may settle in a minute... sometimes it takes longer. The key is not to give up. Keep doing them until you reach inner peace and calm. Below are three simple breathing exercises. Try them all to see which ones you like best. Feel free to use only your favorite or practice all of them. Tailor your practice to your preference.

Belly (or Diaphragmatic) Breathing:

- Imagine you are smelling the roses. Bring your attention to the movement of your belly and feel how the air goes in through your nose, down the air pipe, into the lungs, and then expand your belly.

- Now exhale through your mouth and feel your belly deflate. While exhaling imagine you are slowly blowing on the hot soup(Don't splatter the soup!).

- Feel how your belly moves in and out with inhalation and exhalation.

- If any thoughts come to your mind, let them pass like a cloud in a clear sky. Do not analyze them, do not avoid them, don't judge. Just let them pass like a cloud.

- No matter how dark the cloud looks, it is not going to stay forever.

- Be an observer of your thoughts. And bring your attention back to breath in the belly.

Pursed Lip Breathing:

- Relax your neck and shoulder muscles.

- Keep hand on your heart and breathe in slowly through your nose for two counts, keeping your mouth closed. Do not take a deep breath; a normal breath will do. It may help to count to yourself as you inhale: *one, two.*

- Pucker or purse your lips as if you were going to whistle or gently flicker the flame of a candle.

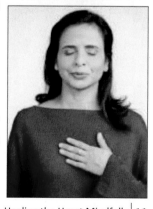

- Breathe out slowly and gently through your pursed lips while counting to four. It may help to count to yourself as you exhale: *one, two, three, four.*

- With regular practice, this technique will become natural to you.

Alternate Nostril Breathing:

- Sit comfortably with your spine erect and shoulders relaxed.

- Put a gentle smile on your face.

- Place your right thumb on your right nostril.

- Press your thumb down on your right nostril and breathe out gently through your left nostril.

- Now breathe in through your left nostril. Press your left nostril gently with your index finger. Remove your right thumb from your right nostril and breathe out from the right.

- Breathe in from your right nostril and breathe out from your left.

- You have now completed one round of alternate nose breathing. Continue inhaling and exhaling from alternate nostrils.

- Complete 9 rounds of alternate breathing through both nostrils.

- After every exhalation, remember to breathe in from the same nostril from which you exhaled.

- Keep your eyes closed throughout. Continue taking long, deep, smooth breaths without any force or effort.

You may find it helpful to add a mantra to your breathing.

Mantra Breathing (optional):

- Say *I am love* or some other soothing and uplifting thought to the rhythm of your breath.

- You can also count while breathing, such as *one, two, three* on the inhale and *one, two, three, four, five on exhale.*

- Softly chant the sacred syllable **AUM** like this ***Ahhhhhhh-ohhhhhhh-mmmmm***. The vibrations have the power to bring about a sense of peace and harmony.

It is hard to go wrong with any of these breathing techniques. Even if you are unsure of the proper technique, just keep practicing and notice how you feel.

Listen to Your Body

Throughout your recovery, the key is to listen to your body more than your mind. If your body tells you to rest, take a rest. If your body signals that it could use some movement, then get up and move.

Your mind has anxieties, fears, worries and judgements that can overshadow the clear messages sent from your body. Much of the mind's communication is emotionally charged so it can create confusion. But if you listen to your body signals and combine them with all the mental knowledge you have, you will heal faster and smoother.

Posture

Posture plays a very important role in recovery. Choose to recommit to good posture throughout the day.

- Stand and sit upright. Be mindful of your back, shoulders, neck, and even eyes.

- Look straight in front of you and see how your vision can help align your neck, thoracic, and lumbar spine (upper and lower back spine).

- Notice if this posture brings you an overall feeling of well-being and confidence.

Gratitude

Remember the blessings in your life and practice these techniques.

- Take a moment for yourself.

- Place a hand on your heart.

- Park all your thoughts aside and focus on taking slow deep breaths.

- Think of one blessing in your life with your eyes closed. It could be anything that feels like a blessing, anything that puts a smile on your face.

- Stay with the thought of that blessing for several breaths.

- Just feel the experience in your heart.

Ahhhh... Isn't it amazing? Choose to believe there is some wisdom or a golden nugget in each and every experience in your life. Every experience or situation you have is for your own personal growth.

The Mindful S.N.A.C.K

To wrap up this section on the tools for mindfulness, I want to offer you a quick and easy way to get mindful in just about any situation. Have a mindful S.N.A.C.K.*

Stop: Stop for a moment.

Notice: Notice what is going on outside and inside with your thoughts, emotions, and feelings.

Accept: Accept the situation and your state of being just as it is without analyzing or judging.

Curious: Get curious about how you want your state of being to be at this moment.

Keep breathing: Keep breathing and see what shifts or opens up.

*The "S.N.A.C.K." is inspired by the work of Carla Naumburg.

S.N.A.C.K in Action

In a session, one of my patients was really upset because he was told that day that he needed to get a pacemaker. I asked him why he was so discouraged and upset. He said he understood intellectually why he needed a pacemaker, but felt that it meant he was regressing. He kept thinking **Why me?** I asked him to try out the S.N.A.C.K principle.

First, I instructed my patient to **S**top and **N**otice what he was going through. He paused and noticed that he was very upset.

Next I encouraged him to **A**ccept completely that he was upset, without analyzing or judging why he was getting a pacemaker and he agreed. He took a deep breath and stopped resisting the idea of getting the pacemaker.

Then I encouraged him to get **C**urious. I asked him how he wanted to feel here and now? He said he obviously wanted to feel calm and peaceful.

Finally, I invited him to **K**eep breathing. He focused on his breath for three minutes without judging and analyzing all the thoughts that were running through his mind.

Guess what opened up during those minutes? My patient became more receptive and calm. He said he felt less upset and a little bit better. I asked him to share one thing that he was grateful for in that moment and he replied: *I am so grateful for the people who invented the pacemaker. Because of them, I will be living more years.*

I was touched and moved by these words. We both just paused and felt that moment of transformation together. Moments like these can only be felt so it is difficult to put into words.

The situation with the pacemaker was the same before doing the S.N.A.C.K work and after. The only thing that changed was the patient's mindset. After S.N.A.C.K, he had a smile on his face. He had transformed his reality by tapping into his own power to change his experience. Unless you try, you just won't know what new experiences might open for you.

SECTION 3

Post Surgery
in the
Hospital

SECTION 3

Post Surgery in the Hospital

Directly after cardiac surgery, you are in the first phase of your recovery. This section will show you how to approach this phase of your healing journey mindfully and address how to handle common post-operative concerns.

Pain Versus Suffering

It is normal to feel physical pain and discomfort after surgery. But sometimes fear around pain can cause patients to avoid movement that is necessary for recovery. Mindfulness can help separate physical discomfort from additional suffering caused by the "thinking mind", thereby making it easier to get moving.

The "golden rule" here to remember is:

Pain is inevitable, but suffering is optional.

Do not avoid or block sensations of pain and discomfort. Instead, choose to accept the pain completely. This way you will be able to discern what is inevitable pain and what is optional suffering. In my experience, pain is a major concern for many patients.

I am often asked, What if this pain doesn't go away? Why am I having so much pain? Why is this happening to me? My roommate doesn't have that much pain! How am I going to walk with so much pain? Will the pain be like this when I go home?

These are all valid concerns. But let's dig a little deeper here. What went wrong? What began as a simple sensation of pain, turned into an emotional experience of suffering. The patient created a story that added meaning to pain.

These thoughts about pain are not actually physical pain. They are self-created suffering based on the patient's mindset. **FEAR** is often little more than false evidence appearing real. You choose to believe fear as if it is reality and that choice causes you to suffer. In order to move forward, I encourage you to take conscious action in the face of your fears.

In order to break through the pain, bring awareness to your own breathing pattern. Then choose a breathing technique that will bring you relief. Breathing is a phenomenal way to help you break through pain and discomfort (see Mindful Breathing section). Once you have done this breath work, you will likely start to feel a little bit better. Now ask yourself: Is the pain *intolerable?*

If the answer is Yes, check with your nurse to see if you are due for pain medicine and request for it. If the pain is tolerable, then continue the breath work while also becoming aware of your mindset.

Get present to things around you, like,

- If there are flowers, admire their beauty.

- Enjoy the view from your window.

- Do a gratitude exercise.

- Count your blessings.

Make sure your are bringing attention to the breath while doing them.

No matter what thoughts come in, accept them completely. Do not analyze them, do not judge them, do not ignore them. All you need to do is accept them and bring your focus back to the breath.

Change your position. Move or walk a little bit while doing your breath work. If you have tubes or lines, ask a nurse or physical therapist to assist you. Always make an attempt to do exercises and ambulate if your pain is tolerable.

Scientific research supports these alternative methods for alleviating pain and discomfort. You will be amazed by how much power you feel when you are able to differentiate between pain and suffering. Choose not to be consumed with suffering.

These are the first few steps to break through the pain. Follow them and you will no longer be a victim of pain and discomfort. Instead, you will be a victor who accepts pain and finds the best way to move beyond it.

Movement and Rest

Some cardiac post-operative patients are nervous about movement and exercise. They are unsure when to move, and when to rest. This can cause them to either want to take it easy all the time or overdo it.

After you have had a big surgery, it is important to find the right balance of movement and rest. It is natural that you will want to rest. However it is also crucial to exercise for your recovery. If you did not have any physical impairments before surgery, there should be no reason to have any physical difficulty ambulating or exercising after surgery.

If there is any medical reason not to exercise, the physical therapist and team will defer your treatment sessions. No one wants you to have any problems. However, re-introducing movement should be approached in a balanced way.

During your hospital stay, do gradual exercises. Less intense, but more frequently. The rehab professionals and other team members will guide you through the recovery process.

Movements Coordinated with Breathing

By coordinating movements with breath, the movements become more comfortable. Simple, conscious breathing in and out while getting in and out of a chair or bed, up from the toilet seat, or walking will make a huge difference in mobility.

If you hold the breath, you are in a contracted state and your muscles become tight. But if you are breathing with movement, you are in an expansive state and will find freedom in whatever you are doing. When coordinating breath with movement, pain is reduced. You are also more likely to use proper body mechanics so you do not compensate in other areas. You will thereby maintain good alignment and posture.

Just remember not to hold your breath while doing any movements. A simple way to remember this is to wear a SMILE on your face. You will never hold your breath if you are smiling. Even if it's a pretend smile, it still works.

Avoiding Comparison and Trusting the Process

Sometimes post-operative patients get stuck with their recovery because they are comparing themselves to other patients or to how life was before surgery. Instead of doing this, choose to be present in your own experience and trust your unique healing journey.

It is good to do research and gather information about post-op recovery, but do not let what you have learned get you stuck in ideas of what your recovery should look and feel like. Be aware and alert of other patients experiences, but do not keep worrying what if that happens to *me?* Or what if my recovery doesn't go well as his?

Sometimes patients won't move forward because they are stuck in the memory of the pain they felt the first day after surgery. They fear that the pain will be the same even though it is now the third day after surgery. They are in a past memory of pain, which delays their present recovery.

Each and every moment is a NEW moment in your recovery. The truth is, in this new moment you might have a completely different experience. You might be much more capable than you think. For example, if you are driving a car, do you only look in the rear view mirror? If you do, what happens? You will have a collision and stop moving.

Recovery is the same. Your experience the day after surgery is in your rearview mirror. You do not need to dwell. Do not let that first day limit your second and third days. Instead, learn from it and move forward. When you start from the present moment, you have space to create a new future.

Mindfulness Beyond Recovery

After practicing mindfulness with a patient during his physical therapy session, the patient got into the habit of being mindful in other situations. This made everything about his hospital stay much easier. Here is what he reported:

Yesterday when I called my nurse twice and she didn't show up right away, I caught myself getting irritated and angry. But since doing the mindfulness work with you in physical therapy sessions, I knew I had a choice about my experience; to react impulsively or to respond mindfully.

I anchored my attention on my breath and for the first time I became aware of the power I have in any given situation. I can choose not to be angry or irritated if the nurse doesn't come right away. While focusing on my breath, I realized that I am in a hospital setting and my nurse has other patients besides me. Who knows if they are having an emergency situation? I became more compassionate for others.

While I was waiting for my nurse, I stayed present with my breath and focused on the beautiful view outside my window. When the nurse came, I had gratitude for her for taking care of me and helping me in my recovery phase. And she noticed and acknowledged me for my patience. It was like I had set a new tone that affected the whole space.

Preparing for Home

Many of my patients say *I feel very comfortable in the hospital. I am happy to go home, but I am nervous about managing at home without the team of professionals. How will I comb my hair? How will I reach the top shelf of my cabinet with sternal precautions?*

A frequent concern of cardiac patients is that they feel comfortable in the hospital, but are nervous about functioning on their own. Anxiety about going home is a very normal feeling. Accept this feeling completely, but do not let it limit your recovery. Do not let it turn you into a victim.

If you are going to a rehabilitation center after your hospital stay, you will be under the supervision of your doctor and interdisciplinary treatment team. No need to worry about being completely independent yet.

If you are heading straight home after your hospital stay, be sure to write down all of your questions before you leave. Make a list of all your concerns. Write down every single thing that comes to mind on a piece of paper. Each and every question that comes to mind is an important one. So instead of searching for the answers in your head, write down those questions during your hospital stay and then ask the experts on your team.

Your doctor or nurse can address your medicine related questions. Your occupational therapist or physical therapist can address anything related to your activities of daily living, functional mobility, and exercise. As your questions are answered, your worries will fade. This way you can use all your energy to heal yourself rather than pouring it into stressful thoughts.

Remember, your entire hospital team is there to make your stay as comfortable as possible. They are also available to help you transition back to your daily life. Do not ever feel bad to call on us for help. We all get paid for what we do. Request and accept our help in making your transition to home as stress-free as possible.

After you're discharge home and you've more questions or concerns, don'
forget that we are all just a phone call or email away. If you still feel anxiou
about going home, do not analyze or judge those thoughts. Instead, focus o
the present moment and do your breath exercises.

Take a few gentle deep breaths and observe your thoughts slow down. It'
time to make your understanding an experience.

Pause again, take a few gentle deep breaths..... now let's move on to th
next session.

SECTION 4

Going Home
and
Other Concerns

Going Home and Other Concerns

When it is time to go home, make sure you are clear on all instructions given by your hospital team. Take your medications on time and follow all precautions given to you in the hospital.

Exercise and Rest

The next big concern patients often have when going home is exercise and movement.

Wouldn't it be better to wait until I feel better and my pain is under control before I start exercising and walking? What exercises should I do and how much? What if I do something wrong? Which movement should I avoid!

Do not worry. You cannot do anything wrong if you follow the instructions given to you at the time of discharge. Your discharge packet from the hospital will have instructions with do's and don'ts. Follow those instructions. But most importantly LISTEN TO YOUR BODY.

This means if your body says I am tired today, take a rest. Do not heed worrisome thoughts that say if you don't exercise your surgery will fail. At the same time, beware of laziness or fear as an excuse not to exercise. Sometimes fearful thoughts will tell you to just keep resting because you had a big surgery, when in fact you are fit to exercise.

Listen to the cues from your body. This is the key to discerning when to exercise and when to rest. Here is the best way to decide between avoiding exercise and overdoing it. If you are tired and don't feel like exercising, tell yourself *I am going to try once.* Your exercise could be as simple as just getting out of bed or walking a few steps. If you still feel tired, don't continue. But if you feel like you can do more, continue the exercises.

Always warm up and cool down before and after exercises and pace yourself during the exercise. Every activity you do is considered an exercise. For example, if you take a shower, that is an exercise. So after a shower you might need to take a rest for couple of minutes; not hours. Then you could do some breathing and go for a walk or do any other set of exercises.

As you approach your exercises, remember if there was no problem with your legs or hands prior to cardiac surgery, you should not see them as limitations in your recovery. If you were unable to walk because of shortness of breath, your breathing should be improved now and you will be able to walk better.

Sometimes patients think, *I didn't have any problem walking before so I don't need to walk or exercise my legs after surgery. But walking is not just for your legs. It is a gradual conditioning of your heart after surgery.*

Dealing with Home Demands

What if I don't have time to do my exercises because I am so busy with kids, home, and work? Another common concern from post-operative patients is, I don't have time for myself. I have small kids and I have to get back to work. How will I have time to exercise or practice mindfulness when I get home?

My question to you is: If you don't have money, can you lend it to someone else? It is the same with self-care. If you are not able to take care of yourself, how do you plan to give care to others?

By taking care of yourself and making time for yourself, you will be more fulfilled. Then you can give quality time and care to others, such as your kids, family, friends, and coworkers more effectively. Let your surgery be a wake up call to prioritize your own self-care.

Complete Healing

Sometimes I hear from post-op patients, *Will I ever feel better after this big surgery? I need assistance for just going to the bathroom, walking and getting out of bed. Will I really be able to heal completely?*

This brings me back to the importance of your mindset. You should not hope, but believe in yourself and focus on the most positive outcome. Keep choosing to be the creator of your experience.

The recovery period is just a phase of pain, discomfort, soreness, and occasionally not feeling well. Remember, these are all physical sensations. Please do not build up a fearful story and add suffering through worrisome emotions.

Surgeons, doctors, nurses and therapists... anybody from your team cannot make you feel better unless you want to feel better. The power is within you. Your medical team did their part and now it's your turn to take responsibility and become the primary factor in your recovery.

Choose an optimistic mindset. Look at the bigger picture and imagine your beautiful life ahead. Keeping a positive, hopeful mindset will give you the strength for the natural ups and downs that come with the recovery phase and life.

My Vision - A New You

Happiness is a choice, not a result. Nothing will make you happy until you choose to be happy. Happy people create their own happiness. They do not wait around for life to do it. The truth about happiness is that it comes from within us and moves outward, not the other way around.

Wayne Dyer offers one of my favorite quotes on happiness. He says, *"There is no way to happiness; rather happiness is the way."*

Robert Holden offers, "We can chase happiness or choose happiness - it depends on how much time we want to save."

To inspire your own happiness, regularly count your blessings (*see the Gratitude Exercise). Make new friends in the hospital, be present to the view from your room, look at the artwork displayed on the walls if you are ambulating in the hallway.

As you move around, notice your own feelings and acknowledge others if they have put a smile on your face, or have made you feel special in any way. Do not take anything for granted; the people who have helped you or your loved ones. Choose to express your gratitude and positive feelings.

Always remember:

What you think, you become.
What you feel, you attract.
What you imagine, you create.

Surgeons and doctors can add years to your life by doing the surgery and treating you. But you as a patient can add life to years. If you take one step, the universe will take 100 steps to support you. Whatever challenges life brings, in physical or mental form, see how they can make you stronger and teach you how to grow in your own beautiful life.

Conclusion

If you have reached this point, congratulations! You have completed th most important first step in becoming the architect of your healing journe Wow! Getting ready to try something new, like mindfulness, shows you ar ready to take ownership of your mindset and your positive recovery.

If you are already practicing mindfulness, I assure you that utilizing thes practices as part of your post-operative recovery will take you to an eve broader level of awareness. If you are a novice, you will likely be inspired t use these practices in your day-to-day life as well. Moment by moment, yo will realize that you can use mindfulness to consciously create the life yo want to live. This will mark the beginning of new possibilities for expansio in your world.

Having done this practice for several years now, I still discover somethin new every day. I am at a stage where I feel like I know myself and I do nc know myself at the same time... because who I am keeps expanding.

Every day I experience the possibility of greater presence and possibility i my life. The more I practice, the more I love this work. Looking back now, wonder how I lived without mindfulness.

For your own optimal recovery, I suggest that you read this book once, the slowly read it again while practicing each tool. As you practice the tool: share your experience with your friends, loved ones, other patients, or wit whosoever else you come in contact. By regularly sharing with others, soo you will not have to read what is written in the book anymore. You will hav your own experiences which will inspire you to keep practicing mindfulness

If this book doesn't resonate with you, I encourage you to just do th S.N.A.C.K exercise. Stop, Notice and Accept the feeling or thought, ge Curious, Keep breathing. Whatever opens up, experience it.

Do not give this book the power to make you feel upset. YOU are the creato of your happiness. Stay present with your power and smile. If the message and practices in this book have resonated with you, you know what to dc Just add to the practices a bit of faith.

Choose to have faith in yourself and the creator of all of us. We are each bor with the capacity to have faith that everything happens for a reason. We ca choose faith that everything will be okay in the end and if it is not okay, th next moment will be a new moment and a new beginning!

This book will help you complete your recovery phase in a very powerful way. Mindfulness practices can mark the beginning of your NEW LIFE, the empowered life you always wanted. My best wishes and love are there with you in every moment of your recovery phase and beyond. You deserve the best in your life!

Testimonial - Mindfulness Post Surgery and Beyond

I was a patient at one of the best hospitals for my open heart surgery and I spent my recuperative time both in the Cardiac ICU and the Cardiac Unit where I had the pleasure of having Monica Jain as my acute care physical therapist.

From the very first unwilling baby steps, to longer walks with the walker, to working with stairs, to finally being able to walk unaided, Monica was there to prompt and encourage me every step of the way.

Beyond the physical therapy, she was an inspiration to me then and forever in the emotional balance needed through the mindfulness approach. I continue to try to breathe in the good and breathe out the bad, so to speak, and I am reminded of her words as we slowly walked and talked in this regard.

My experience there was not only the physical aspects, but a fuller approach which I'll sum up as her "mindfulness" approach. I want to thank her for care during my hospital stay and for the positive spirit that she infused in me with her multifaceted approach.

About My Journey, This Book, and My Ongoing Work

As you now know, mindfulness practices transformed my life. By offering these practices to my family, we now share a very different bond as compared to before. Inspired by that, I started to integrate these principles into the physical therapy work I do with my patients.

Helping my patients become victors in their recovery is deeply fulfilling. I feel an expansion in my heart that is so profound, I cannot even put it into words. Following the advice of my mentors, colleagues, and patients, I chose to open up and share the beloved work in this book with you.

But it doesn't stop here. I am now bringing mindfulness awareness to my community. Companies and universities regularly invite me to speak and share my insights on mindfulness. The need for this work is so great that more people keep wanting to learn more. Whenever I think this is it and I am all done, I am reminded by these words from my editor - there is always next step! This is true. When you complete one step, the universe always offers the next step.

When I look back on my own teaching journey, I am so grateful. I am grateful for the grace of this wonderful universe and our creator for choosing me as an instrument to share this message of mindfulness. It is my honor and privilege to have curious readers like you who want to take ownership of their lives. It inspires me to connect with people who want to be active creators of every experience of their lives.

Welcome, welcome, and welcome to this beautiful journey, where you get to design every moment as you truly wish!

APPENDIX

Post Surgery Physical Therapy

APPENDIX

Post Surgery Physical Therapy

During your hospital stay you will be educated on:

- Techniques to protect your chest bone to allow for optimum healing.

- Safe mobility with or without assistive devices.

- Pacing and energy conservation for your daily activities.

- Individualized home exercise program.

Mindfulness can fit in beautifully with all of the above. While doing your exercises, take a moment to check in with yourself and see if you are present in the moment. If you are, wonderful. If not, I recommend using one of your favorite mindfulness tools to come back to the present moment. Once you feel settled and present, proceed with the exercise.

Sternal Precautions

The purpose of sternal precautions is to keep your body in the best possible position for healing after surgery. So it is important to be careful with how you use your arms after surgery. Here are techniques to protect your chest bone to allow for optimum healing.

- Do not lift more than ten pounds for three months.

- Avoid pulling, pushing, or stretching through your arms.

- Limit any strenuous overhead movement with your arms. Bring one arm at a time behind your head or behind your back when needed.

- Avoid placing pressure on arms to support/lift your body. Place hands on thigh/knee instead of on an armrest when going from sit to stand.

- Do not let others pull or grab your arms under your armpit when they are helping you.

Heart Pillow

You will be given a soft heart-shaped pillow after your surgery.

- When coughing, sneezing, and laughing, hold your heart pillow against your chest with both arms.

- Support your chest with your heart pillow while sitting down and standing up.

Sleeping

- You will want to sleep on your back or side for a few weeks.

- Use as many cushions or pillows as you need to make your body comfortable.

- If you prefer sleeping in a recliner chair initially, that is fine too.

Riding in a car

- You'll need to ride in the backseat for a few weeks to avoid air bag deployment in case of collision.

- Do not drive for at least six weeks.

If at any time you notice clicking or cracking along your sternum, report to your doctor or surgery team right away. Remember, you do not have to memorize any of the precautions right now. You will be reminded repeatedly of these precautions by your rehab and medical team when you are in the hospital. Plus you will be given a reference guide. Your team will make sure that you master all of them before you go home.

Exercise Overview

Here you will find typical post cardiac surgery physical therapy exercises. You do not need to memorize these exercises. **Your hospital team will design the exercise program based on your medical condition.** This section is simply a reference on how recovery exercises can be paired with mindfulness.

Each person's healing journey is unique. Do not compare yourself with the experience of others. Do not compare your yesterday with today. Every day is different in the initial recovery phase.

Hospital Exercise Program

In the hospital, your rehabilitation will be focused on these goals:

- Simple physical exercises in different positions (lying in bed, sitting in a chair, standing) tailored to your body and fitness level.

- Breathing exercises to gradually expand your lungs.

- Functional Activities (getting in and out of bed, getting up and down from a chair, walking, getting in and out of car, and stair climbing).

Day 1

You are out of anesthesia, awake, and ready to exercise. Depending on your medical condition, your team will decide whether you are ready to get out of bed. If you are not getting out of bed, here are some exercises to do in bed

Bed Exercises:

- **Gratitude Exercise:** Put one hand over your heart, close your eyes, and think about anything you feel grateful for in the present moment. Notice how the energy inside you shifts as you feel your gratitude.

- **Ankle pumps:** Move your ankles towards and away from you by pointing and flexing your feet. Do five to ten repetitions every one to two hours when you are awake. This is a nice simple way to loosen up your joints and increase circulation throughout your body while lying in bed.

Knee caps: Repeatedly push your knees down into the mattress and firm your knee caps. Do five to ten repetitions every one to two hours when you are awake. This is a way of preparing your quadricep muscles to prime you to get out of bed and get moving again.

Belly Breathing: Put one hand on your belly and take slow, gentle breaths, moving your belly out and in. This will expand your lungs, increase the volume of your breath, and calm your nervous system. Do at least five repetitions every one to two hours when you are awake.

Incentive Spirometer/Flutter: These are breathing devices that will help you loosen up secretions in your lungs to breathe more deeply. Your physical therapist or nurse will teach you how to use these devices.

Chair Exercises:

If you are getting out of bed and into a chair with the help of your team, add these chair exercises. To maintain mindfulness, keep your focus on breathing in and out while doing them. All of these exercises will prepare you to start walking again.

- **Ankle Pumps:** Start with both feet flat on floor. Lift and lower your heel off the floor. Then lift and lower your toes up and down.

- **Marching:** Start with both feet on floor. Lift one foot up and put it back down. Then repeat the same with the other foot. Start with ten repetitions and progress to twenty.

- **Knee flexion and extension (seated leg kicks):** Start with both feet on floor. Lift your foot completely until your knee is straight, slowly bring it back down. Then try it with your other leg. Start with ten repetitions and progress to twenty.

- **Belly breathing:** Put one hand on your belly and take slow, gentle breaths. Move your belly out and in. Do at least five repetitions. Notice how you feel.

- **Incentive Spirometer:** This breathing device will help you breathe more deeply. Your physical therapist or nurse will teach you how to use it.

- **Gentle arm movements:** Start with your hands by your sides, raise one hand up in front of your face and slowly bring it back down. Repeat with other hand. Start with ten repetitions and progress to twenty.

Day 2

Continue with Day 1 exercises and progress to the next level. Depending on your rehab team's decision, you may start walking. Walk according to their instructions. Your specific regimen will depend on your endurance and medical condition. Practice your mindfulness by consciously breathing with every step you take.

Day 3 and beyond

Now you're getting closer to your time of discharge. Your rehab team will continually assess your condition to progress your exercises. Progression includes building endurance for exercises, walking, and climbing stairs to gradually condition your heart and optimize your recovery. If you have been cleared to get in and out of bed and up and down from bed on your own, follow these key points for movement.

Moving in bed:

- Lower your legs over the side of the bed.

- Hold your heart pillow while you sit upright at the edge of bed.

- Keep the movement coordinated with breathing.
- Sit at the edge of the bed for a few seconds before getting up.

Going to the chair:

- Walk to the chair.
- Feel the chair with your legs. If it is a recliner chair on wheels, make sure the chair is locked.
- Reach for the arm of the chair for gentle support.
- Slowly lower yourself down with one hand touching the arm of the chair and the other hand holding your heart pillow close to your sternum.
- Sit down very slowly while breathing out. (Imagine you are blowing on hot soup).
- Scoot yourself all the way back in the chair slowly by sliding your hips back, one side at a time.
- Once you are all the way back, put a pillow support in place if needed or ask somebody to do that for you.

Going to the bed:

- Grab your heart pillow and squeeze it against your chest. Or place both hands on your lap.
- Scoot/slide your hips forward to edge of chair.
- Position your feet flat on the floor underneath your knees and gently rock for momentum.
- Lean forward and use your legs to push down and stand up.
- Avoid bearing weight on your arms to get up. Lean forward.
- Coordinate all movements with your mindful breathing.

Leaving the hospital:

If you are going home, your hospital/rehabilitation team will provide you with a written home exercise program tailored to your recovery, home environment, and medical status. The rehab team will answer all questions related to your mobility and recovery from the rehab perspective.

If you are prescribed a home physical therapist, then you will receive guidance at home regarding your rehab and recovery. If you are discharged to a facility, then the rehab team at the facility will guide you during your stay.

Going home in an automobile:

- Turn so your back side faces the seat with your feet facing the door.

- Slowly sit down while holding your heart pillow across your chest. Bend your knees and stick your bottom out to lower down.

- Reverse these steps to get out of the car.

- Make sure you are coordinating all the movements with slow deep breaths. Refrain from holding your breath.

- Use a pillow across your chest to help prevent seat belt irritation.

- Do not sit in the front passenger seat for six weeks.

Home Exercise Program

These exercises can be done with the walking program. Do these exercises 3 times a day for 10-15 repetitions, depending on how you feel. (Refer to previous section for further explanation).

- Ankle pumps

- Knee flexion and extension (seated leg kicks)

- Marching

- Breathing exercises

- Incentive spirometer/Flutter

Walking:

In the initial period of recovery, walking is the best choice of exercise. Walking will recondition your heart and your whole body after surgery.

- Consistency is key. Find the best time of day that works for you and walk on a regular basis.

- Walk on level ground in the beginning.

- Wear comfortable clothing and footwear that feels good on your feet.

- Avoid extreme temperatures. Walk indoors if it is too cold or hot outside.

- Start off slow. Then increase to your regular walking pace. Slow down again to end the walk.

- If you feel too tired during your walk, take a rest. Walk again when you feel ready. Check in with yourself regularly.

- If you experience any abnormal symptoms during your walk, such as nausea, chest pain or jaw pain, stop and contact your doctor.

- Do not walk immediately after a big meal.

Week 1 - Frequent walks, short duration. For example, 5 minute walk, 4-5 times per day.

Week 2 - Less frequent walks, longer duration. For example, 8-10 minute walk, 2-4 times per day.

Week 3 - Follow the same rule of reducing frequency and increasing duration. For example, 12-15 minute walk, 2-3 times per day.

Weeks 4-12 - When you have reached the duration of a 20 minute walk once a day, include both a warm up and cool down period. Eventually progress to 30 minutes once a day.

Week 12 - You may be eligible for an outpatient cardiac rehab program. Check with your team and get more information.

Please notify your doctor right away or call 911 if you experience any of the following symptoms:

- Excessive pressure in your chest, shoulder, arms, neck, jaw.

  Shortness of breath or racing and pounding of your heart rate while at rest.

- New weakness in your extremities or vision changes.

KEY POINTS FOR ME

KEY POINTS FOR ME

KEY POINTS FOR ME

Made in the USA
Middletown, DE
31 March 2021